IMPRINTS

MANKIND'S IMPRESSION ON HISTORY

BHAGWAT SHARAN GOYAL

ISBN 979-888591019-4

Contents

Prologue

Born in Brijbhumi, Land of the Lord, Dr. Bhagwat Sharan Goyal is one of the most highly educated people in India. as an educationalist, he has worked in various capacities in and outside the country. He is a widely travelled man, covering not only the whole of India, from Leh Sri Nagar to Kanya Kumari Dwarka to Imphal, but also to most parts of the world.

He can boast of setting foot on 6 of 7 continents. As a great patron of Sports and Cultural Activities he's affiliated to many NGOs. He's a great philanthropist in his own order, and writes in leading newspapers.

"Imprints" is a tribute to those who tried to make our lives 'Sublime' at best and bashful at worst. More than five thousand years of civilization are indebted to the most towering figures, and the events that resulted from the omissions and commissions of mankind.

Though some tragic and some beautiful, all of them have left their imprints on the terrain of time, always leading to one another step in civilization, and one step further into the void of time.

Some generous, some villainous, all are inseparable from the existence of homo sapiens. Good cannot be distinguished without the presence of evil, likewise a goblet of nectar cannot be comprehended without a vial of poison. Their actions and reactions make life what it is.

Time has thus given us our most important artifact: destiny. Time and Destiny both never look back. Therefore, these imprints become the hallmark of our civilization and lead mankind into an unknown future.

Therefore, a wise man is one who likes his lamp, without making a fuss of the dark.

- B.S. Goyal

God, Religion And Soul

It Was In The Sixth Millennium

Savior Krishna Came To Earth

In This Deep Sonorous Voice

Preached Us All What Life Is Worth

Mortals Have To Play Their Part

Fit For Them Or Not To Suit

The Only Way To Surge Ahead

Duty, With Out Hope Of Fruit

Soul, Not Body Matters Much

Only Yogi's Have It Thought

The World Is Too Much With Us

The Only Theory We Have Bought

~.~

Life Is Really A Walking Shadow

Only A Way To Decreed Door

Guided By The Deeds Of Dare

Ending At The Oceanic Shore

Soul The Everlasting Source

Natural Forces Work And Work

Burning, Blowing, Ravaging, Rusting

Fail To Give It The Slightest Jerk

Body Serves As Clothing Kind

Death, A Temporal Life Station

Hold The Stores For Change Of Clothing

Move Affresh To New Nestation

The Wheel Of World Is Moving On

With Birth And Growth To Decay And Death

Nurse By Nature On Its Part

In Varied Moods Of Rig And Wrath

So Love For Life Is Love For Karm

Not To Live By Roary Past

The Only Way To Keep Alive

Doing Duty Till The Last

Treat The World As Yogi's Do

Duty's Deity Be The Motto

Karm Without Hope And Fear

Gain Or Loss Or Love Or Lotto

'fond To A Fault' Is The Route To Ruin

For All The World To Kiss

With The Passion Like A Yogi

Search Eternal Divine Bliss

Perils In Pain, Suffering And Shame

Nature's Wrath Are Lot Of Earth

But Love Of God For Every Creature

'nables One To Cross The Dearth.

~.~

He Sent A Dream To Noah The Great,

That Future Floods Will Swallow The Earth

That Saving Creation Was His Duty

Blessed Be To Wisdom Worth.

Blessed Noad To Will Of God

Designed A Long And Burly Arch

Packed With Seeds And Pairing Creatures

Alert And Ready To Face The Dark

Deluge, Then Visited As Was Warned

Lifting Slowly The Blissful Arch

Midst The Rain For 40 Twins

Ceaseless Lash And Creeping Dark

Water Her And Water There

Water, Water Everywhere

In Leaping Water, Pouring Rain

Noah's Ark, A Sight So Rare

Floating Till One Fifty Days

Mount Ararat Came To Site

Receding Waters Left The Land

Earth Against Saw Day And Light

For Faith, And Duty And Full Patients

Coupled With Ringing Common Sense

Noah Was Titled Grandest Sire

Godly Will Leaves No One Tense

~.~

Abraham Aged Ninety Nine

Got The Message Right Divine

Give Me The Dearest Thing Of Yours

To Save The World From Satanic Line

With Faith So Deep And Faith So Wide

Isaac As The Dearest Bill

A Sacrifice To The Will Of God

They Mounted Up Garulea Hill

With Munching Prayers Closing Ice

Sire's Dagger Rose And Fell

Wonder Struck, With Open Eyes

Gabrael Cast A Sizzling Spell

He Welcomes Him With A Broad Smile

Isaac As A Dutiful Son

A Lamb Was Lying On The Altar

Godly Bid Had Been Done

One Who Made The Earth The Sky

The Sun The Moon The Mount The Valel

Test The Faithful Time To Time

By Sending Rains, Storms And Hail

So Faith And Duty A Hand In Hand

A Clear Message To Mortal Man

Abraham Feared Greatest Band

Of Jewish, Muslim, Christian Clan

~.~

All That Glittered Was Not Gold

Ramses's Egypt Crying Hoarse

Jewish Slave To Harshest Life

No Holds Barring Cruelest Course

Jacob's Genre Adopted Land

Put Heart And Soul In Growing Corn

But Pharaos Anger Rose And Rose

Er Joseph's Service Were For Lorn

Jews Were Made The Meanest Creature

Time To Time, Slave Of Slave

Forced To Work By Day And Night

Worse And Worst They Had To Brave

Rising From The Rank-and-file

Moses Swore To Save Their Grace

Preaching Freedom From Tyranny

Took Rameses Versus Face To Face

'exodus' With Freedom Fever

For The Search Of Promised Lands

Prophet Wandered 40 Years

Getting God's 10 Commands

Piety, Freedom And Fervent Faith

Meekness, Patience, Peace To Crave

Moses The Merciful Taught Us How

Fortune Always Favors The Brave

~.~

Once A Prince While On The Mall

Saw A Sick And Winkled Man

Next A Dead And Dreadful Soul

All This Left And Thoughtful Then

Why Is Sorrow The Lot Of Man?

What Makes Autumn Win Spring

Where To Find Lasting Peace

Sickening Cause Of All Suffering

Soon He Left His Princely Pleasure

Renounced The World For A Final Dip

For Weeks And Months And Years Together

Wandered Like A Rudderless Ship

Under The Oak On Full Moon Night

One Day He Felt A Light In The Dark

'desire' The Cause Of Suffering Found

Check And Feel Your Joyful Arc.

Those Who Love The Fellow Creature

Really Know The Secret Of Life

Loving A Foe Is The Jewel Of Crown

Goal Of 'nirvan' Guess Is Rife

Lying, Slander, Abuse Lang,

Compounded With Useless Talk

The Four Sin Sof Speech Together

Push Man From Good To Balk.

Right Beliefs, And Words And Thinking

Deeds And Deals And Always Chest

Efforts And Ideals All Together

Pave The Path But, Not In Haste

Knowing The Self To Rid Of Sufferings

Always Wins The Worldly Game

Showing The Righteous Path Of Light

'blessed Buddha', The Prince Became

~.~

Lao-tze Came Into The World To Worship

Viewed The Nature' 'o Clan

Life Is The Stretch Of 'tao'l

Eternal Truth For Real Man

Rising Start Of East In Wisdom

Gleams Of Goodwill And Holy Plan

'do To Others What Hope To Be Done'

He Laid The Golden Rule For Man

Choosing Honest And Right People

Open Secret For Ruler Gracious

Morel, Philosopher Teacher Of Teachers

Bows The World To Great Confucius

Life Is But A Daring Duel

Darting Between Good And Evil

War And Fight To Struggle Rife

Supreme Rank To Make A Kill

Life Is Not A Walking Shadow

Nor Is It A Poor Player

Fire Cleans The Root Of Evil

Said Zoraster Everywhere

~.~

Nature Heralded With A Bang

The Welcome Now The King Of Kings

Bethlehem Was The Town Of Honor

Magies Followed Heavenly Ring

Then Christ Became Anointed Jesus

Always Preached The Love Of God

The Shepherd From The Tent Of Gold

Rears The Sheep On Lovely Sod

It Is He Who Never Sleeps

And Keeps On Ringing Life's Bell

It Is He Who Makes The Giant

Dwarf, The Earth, Heaven And Hell

We Are All Sheep, And He Is The Master

Looks After The Great And Small

Then Why Should We Hate Our Neighbor's Body?

And Shroud The World With Gloom And Pall?

Do Thy Duty To Thy Neighbor

Leave The Rest To His Holy Plant

Faith In Him And Sacred Healing

Smoothly Runs Life's Fan

Jesus Got The Call From Father

Left The World At Youthful Age

Forgive Forget Do The Right Thing

Free From Fear Fretting Rage

~.~

On The Scorching Arabian Sand

Tribals Fought To Run Their Writ

The Poor, Wretched, Comment All

Found Themselves Hardest Hit

Muhammad Rose To Heights Of Prophet

Gave Them Fair United Look

Revealing The Truth From Godly Light

Handed Over The Holy Book

God Is One And A Visible Ray

Looks After One And All

They Are Equal In His Eyes

Whether Big Or Slow And Small

Faith In Him And Grace Is Life

Sacrifice And Charity Same

Color, Race Or Birth No Matter

In This Brothers Worldly Game

Those Who Lead A Holy Life

Think Of Allah All The Time

Find The Gates Of Heaven Open

Nay, The Fire Of Hell To Mine

Kingdoms and Beginnings Of Civilization

Flow Of Nile Never Stops

Er Clans And Genres Rise And Fall

Saints And Sages Kings And Queens

Leave Imprints For Future Calls

Menes, Khufu, Khafre Kings

Khenaton, Tuton, Ramsay's Great

With Silent Sleep And Solemn Faith

Stemmed The Tide To Time's Wait

Sphinx, Pyramids And Hieroglyphs

Mummy, Mortuary, Temple And Tomb

Painted Walls And Masks Of Gold

Karnak, Luxor, Simbel, Somb

Papyrus Writing, Pillars And Combs

Make A Mark By Telling The Tale

Er Human Race Has Traveled Long

All Along The Niles Dale

Mark Of Race And Peace With Time

Faith And Duty With Labor And Fame

Pharaoh's Using The Human Mind

Always Tried To Win The Game

~.~

Flow Of Indus Matched The Nile

In Thoughts Of God And Gifts Of Nature

Whirling Life And Death Together

Time Moves The Soul Of Creature

God Revealed The Vedas Tracing

Answering Questions 'who Am I?"

Whats The Purpose, What Is Life?

Whither I Come To Go And Why

Denying Themselves Worlds Of Pleasure

Mystics, Saints And Numerous Pages

Kept The Torch Of Light Burning

Pace By Pace In All Ages

Jeev And Brahma The Same Divine

Nature Caress Both O Them

Earth Gemmed With Heaven Light

Works To Jeev

As Soothing Sem

Kind And Chaste With Liberal Line

Truth And Love As Walking Rod,

Too Generous, Faithful, Selfless Guy

Serving Man Is Serving God

~.~

Euphrates And Tigris Tantalize,

Base For Culture Human Race

Cradled Kush, Ur, Babylon Like

Sumerian Moved With Fastest Pace

Surplus Food, Division Of Labor

Public Works And Cuneiform

Religion, Teaching, Irrigation

System, Ruler, Law And Norm

Moving First In Wheeler Vehicle

God From Ziggurat Guided Them

War Or Peace Or Testing Times

Glory Acted Like A Sem

‘mmurabi The The Law’, ‘gilmesh The Builder

Might The Power Of Sargon

Brought The Wealth In Peace To Region

Never Before The Humans Don

Mesopotamian And Hanging Garden

Always On The Fore Of Front

First Few Names In The Civilization

Motive Force With Mod Current

~.~

In The Laps Of River Yellow

China Bloomed With Indus Well

Taught The World The Cast Of Bronze

And Made The Temples Ringing Bell

Spinning Silk With Delicacy

Clock The King's With Finest Robe

Working Hard And Tapping Tide

Filled The Belly Of The Mob

Great Strides In Care Of People

Body Puncture First Time Seen

Use Of Leaves And Bark Together

Commons Cured With Interest Keen

Making Paper Gift Of Nature

Raced The Learning Of Every Clan

Gain Of Man And Loss Of Kind

Easy To Jot The And Note The Plan.

All Time Great A Human Venture

One Will Find In China's Wall

Thousands Of Qins In Terracotta

Guarding King At Every Call

~.~

Minoan, Mycenaen In Mediterranean

Raised The Hopes Of World To Come

Heralded Greeks And Roman Forum

Hardy Boards And Palace Plum

From The Home On Mount Olympus

Gods Of Greece Be Moaned Or Blessed

Zeus, Apollo, Aphrodite

Athena, Posei All So Guessed

Sound Body Sound Mind

Hellenic Beauty Be The Pranks

Truth, Must-win And All Attires

Socrates, Plato Led The Ranks

In Polity, Science, Philosophy, Logic

Great Aristotle Left The Mark

People's Rule Awrit Of Solon

Hippo Crates, A Light In Dark

Herodotus, Pythagoras

Prince Of Learning Led The Pace

Arete, Goodness, Love For Life

Filling Greece With Finest Race

Voice Of Zeus 'n Vase Of Venus

Bubbling Life All For Fame

Reigning Fun And Faith Together

Jostling In Olympic Game

Zeus Statue, Artemis Temple

Rhodes Colossus Piece By Piece

Beginnings Of Democracy,

Glittering Glory That Was Greece

~.~

Old Order Changeth

Yielding Place To New

Phoenix Flames Itself

The Rise From Ashes And Dew

Wisdom Of Man And Might Of Mind

Showering Gifts From Godly Home

Coupled With Thoughts Of Hellenic Culture

All Roads Leading Soon To Rome

Republic, Care And Food After All

Columns, Archs And Roads They Chart

Laws, Calendar, Circus Trade

Medical Systems To Lethal Art

Colosseum Forum And Fabulous Bath

Temples, Totem Latin To Cake

Marauding Might Of Their Legions

Made Mediterranean A Roman Lake

Cicero's, Sullas' And Caesar's Reign

Trajan's Lib For Learning Trait

With Government Polity, Platonic Bite

Rome Became A Glory Great

Empires Of Age

Scattered In Some Captured Corners

Moving Like Lonely Stars

Numerous Kingdoms Rose The Tide

Filled The World With Bloody Wars

Hunger, Sickness, Death, And Fear

Tied To Lot Of Common Man

Whim Of Ruler Hit The Heights

Tended, Terror And Frolic Ran

From The Ashes Of Tense Turmoil

Appeared There Cyrus The Great

With Will And Wisdom And Peace And Power

Brought In Order To Tottered State

Land Of Europa And Land Of Light

Craved For Merging In Single-tyre

Groaning, Grieving Mankind Hearing

Rumbles Of A Great Empire

First Time Mankind Had Some Peace,

And First Time Had Defined Laws

Quest For Learning And Jest For Travel

Flew To Freedom From Cruel Jaws

Find Atire Roaring Business

Beauty Of The Big,Big Barge

From The Den Of Persepolis

Rate Of Darius Ran At Large

Finding The World A Copy Of Hell

The Creator Felt Much Geered

Shed A Drop Of Blissful Blood

He Named It Love And Disappeared

~.~

Time, The Great Accounts Keeper

Remains Dishonest, Unrestrained

When And Whose, Cheque Gets Dishonored

All Predictions Fail And Chained

No Leave For Mercy, No Love For Justice

No Like For Appeal No Consideration

Scoffs Of Disdain, Arrogance There

Turns The Man With No Sensation

Blackening Sky Is From The West

And Roaring Rumbles From The East

Icy Winds From North To South

Made The Kingdom Full Of Beasts

With Hordes Of Greek And Flattering Hopes

The Sons Of God's Ran Through The Space

Power, Might And Glea Of Darius

Fell To Pieces And Lost Grace

Charm And Love, Lust For Power

Wealth And Beauty And Pomp Of State

Burning Turrets Of Persepolis

Heralded Hero Alexander The Great

On The Ashes Of Empire

New Ones Saw The Glory Of Greece

Getting Dishonored Cheques From Time

Youth Group Spectre Lay In Peace

Willing His Palms To Be Out Of Wrapping

The Emperor Gave A Quaint Message

Man Comes, Stays And Leaves The World

With Empty Hands To Times Rage

Mauryan's, Gupta's Hans And Chins

Had Great Empires In The East

They Vied To Create A Golden Age

That Differ Man From The Beast

~.~

Spices, Silk And Gorgeous Clothes

Edicts To Regulate Life Of Man

Ashoka The Great Even Banned Hunting

Gave Respite To Harried Clans

Travelers, Traders And Talisman,

Joined Hands For Calm And Peace;

Step-by-step The Race Of Man

Was Marching Onwards Land And Seas

Romans Took The Relay With The Baton

Pushed The Greeks And Ran With Zest,

Rome With Home Of Hooives And Genius,

Lone Empire In The West.

~.~

Land Of Judah Blessed Israel,

Reeled To Giant Goliaths Might;

Gurgling, Fuming, Fretting Horror,

Dared Them To Match In Fight.

All Door Shut And Muted Voice

None Would Face His Wild Power.

Reign Of Terror Lashing Tight,

Heap Of Insults Were Only Showered.

Giant's Roaring Day And Night,

Made Life A Hellish Lay.

Shock, And Shame, And Fear Alike

Ruled The Roost In Dreadful Day.

Tiny David, The Loveliest Child,

Asked Terror To Leave The Land;

The Giant Laughed With Hateful Leer,

Shook The Heavy Club In Hand

~.~

With Blinding Rage The Giant Rushed,

To Smite The Nimble, Gentle Boy;

Pulling The String Of Sling Together,

David Hurled A Stone With Joy!

The Whistling Missile Did Not Miss,

It Hit The Giants Right Eye,

With Shock And Pain In Rush And Tandem,

Brought A Deafening Roar And Cry.

Grunts And Roars And Hoarsing Cries,

Volley Of Shots On Giants Head,

Brought The End To Fatal Fight,

Felled The Giant Goliath Dead.

Faith In Him And Sense Of Pride,

Makes The Small And Powerful Mate,

Sing His Praise And Ask For Mercy,

Keep In Mind That God Is Great!

David In Turn Became The King,

End United The Hebrew Band,

Which To Build A Temple To God,

But Failed, For Wars And Blood Were On Hand

When End Was Near All Was Clear,

Solomon The Son Saw Pain In Eyes,

He Promised The Temple, End To Fight,

Then Sir Blessed Him And Bade Goodbye

Shine Like The Brightest Sun,

And Sing Life's Sweetest Song

Even Among The Tryst Times,

Blessed May You Live, Life Long

For Piety, Peace With Promise And Grace;

For Love And Life And Wisdom Of State;

For Gifts And Gleans To Law & Justice;

Still Remember Solomon The Great

Thinkers

Thinkers Moved From Place To Place,

And Left Behind The Rare Treatise;

Changed The World With Band Or Whisperer,

Making Mankind Worldly Wise.

Vishnu's 'arth' And 'vellis 'prince',

The Finest Works Of Ruling Craft;

Good Of People, Lover Of Ruler,

Peace With Nature, A Final Draft.

How Lovable How Creative,

'utopia' Of Thomas More!

Heaven, Jannat, Swarg Together,

Shadows Work In Days Of Yore

Nostradamus The Mystic Sire,

Brought In Lasting Prophecies;

What To Talk Of Fear And Favor,

Set To Give Us 'centuries'

Hobbes And Locke And Rousseau Thinking,

Social Contract Governing Plan;

Give And Take For Ruled And Ruler

Way To Redeem Our Rattled Clan;

Man May Born Free Anywhere,

But Will Always Find Chains;

Freedom Dumped In Mid Of Mire,

Mourns With Mortal Wounds And Pain.

~.~

Not Many Thousand Years Ago,

The Earth Was Teemed With The Sweetest Grapes;

Men And Women Were Not Found,

Darwin Says 'we Came From Apes'.

To Markx The World Is Not At Peace,

Is Very Much Like A Darkling Plain;

Struggle Rules The Roost Of Matter,

Ignorant Classes Fight In Vain

Freud The Psycho Geographer,

Mapped The Mind In Sub-states.

Color The Dreams Of Beggars Even,

Sex Is Driving Forces For All Mates

Then Nietze Thundered Like A Knight,

Denouncing The Equality Of Man;

Supreme Race Is Always Right,

In Making It A Ruling Clan.

Far From The Maddening Thesis,

Wondered Gandhi From The Fence;

Even The Meanest Has The Right,

To Live With Grace And Honored Sense.

Thinkers Gave Us Thought So Wide,

So Vast Out Of Reach Of Sky,

Broke The Boundaries Of The Nation,

Leaving People To Endless Why.

Conquering The World

Ravage World By Tribal Wars,

Moaned For Long With Deep Scars;

Cried For Peace And Order Far,

The Kings And Queens On Ruthless Czars

Eastern World Saw A Show Called The Great,

With Peace And Order For Five Decades;

Non Violence A Lasting Creede,

Fill The World With Hopeful Rays

Ming's And Hans And Guptas Ring,

Kanishka Lung With Meigi Rose;

Casting The World In Caring Mode,

Mixing Matter In Spiritual Hose.

Byzantium With Hadrian's Rome,

Persian King Arthur Ardasher's Rise;

Court Of Arthur Bettfold Brave,

With Rolland Had A Europe Wise.

Charlemagne Crowned By Pope,

Heralded Middle Ages Repose;

Bravery, Beauty To Fighting Force,

Came To Stay As Lasting Course.

Then Came The Age Of Excellence,

Virgin Queen To Peter The Great;

Caliph Al Rashid To Suleiman Sage,

Mighty Mughals In Albar's Fate.

But All That Glittered Was Not Gold,

In Many Of Rulers Hideous Head.

Ivan The Terrible To Mary's Mess,

Henry The 8th To Catherine Med.

~.~

Attila The Hun, The Scourge Of God,

Changaiz, Halaku As Mangol Might;

With Taimur Crushed The People Alike,

Left The Man Bereft Of Light.

Pizarro Of Spain The Conquistador,

Raiders Like Herman Cortes;

Ruined The Inca And Aztecs,

With Deceit And Cunning In Evil Forte

All Them Tried To Leave The Filth,,

And Heaps Of Torture Humans Bones;

Taking Delight In Sins And Sneer,

Greatest Slaughter, Cries And Moans.

Search Of New World Paved The Way,

For People's Rule In Various Part;

American March With Spangled Banner,

Speeded World's Ongoing Cart.

.

Change The Guard As Washington Knight,

Lincoln's Freedom To Tortured Slaves;

A Martyr For The Cause And Care

American Land For Free And Brave.

Fourteenth Louis' Longest Rule,

To Magnify The Mighty Friends;

Paved The Way For Bloody Bathing,

Napoleon Then Took The Lance.

His Armies March To Overrun Europe,

Sent Chills To Neighboring Lands;

Death Beat Life With Famine And Fire,

Made It Run Like Weary Bands.

Peace Prevailing This Turmoil,

Brought On Rail The Human Race;

Stars Of Freedom Twinkle Together,

New Challenges Where To Face.

Italian Leader Garibaldi,

German Might In Prince Bismarck;

Queen Victoria A Torch Of Light,

New Europe In Dazzling Arch.

Russo's Land In Cromwell's Cadre,

Raced Along With Kaiser's Plan;

To End The World In Slavish Care,

Asian Ace To African Plan.

World At War

For Selfish Nature Of Imperial Powers,

World Witnessed The Horrors Of War;

Millions Muted Mortals Cried,

See This First But Lasting Scar

Death Of Dance In Every Corner,

Heaprs Of Dead On Every Field;

Linking Ruin And Rod Together,

Vied For Kill As Greatest Yield.

Machines Gained Fodder From Human Life,

Satan Had The Bloodiest Thrust;

Nature Moaned And Venus Cried,

Seeing Science At Its Worst.

~.~

East To West And North To South,

Ignorant Armies Fought In Dark;

Hailing Horrors, Faith And Fire,

Father Got A Mortal Mark.

Count Of Corpse Was Lost Forever,

When The Order Got A Change,

Villains And Heroes Worked Together,

Agreed For A New Slavish Range.

Peace And Piety Lost Forever,

Resistive Nature Came To Fore;

Blood Grew Cold With Self And Pride,

Every Hand Was Full Of Gore.

~.~

Sleeping Lion Had A Stir,

Zulu Chaka Led The Charge;

Sand Of Sahara Settling Down,

But Thickening Clouds Looming Large.

Caliph's Had The Ash To Bite,

Ataturk Pasha Rose From Dust;

Whims Of King To World Of People,

Old Empire Lost The Crust

Yatsen Kept Hopes Alive,

To Free The Dragon From This Net;

Lenin Through The Czar's Aside,

Soaking Russia With With Bloody Bet.

Wilson's Voice Vain In Wagon,

Versailles To Get A Name;

Future, Terror, Horror, Bearer,

Root Of Tragic Germs That Came

Bolivar Simon Brought A Thesis,

Led A Churning In Latin Lands;

Sleeping Lion Dumped In Dungeon,

Moaned And Cried In Rule Of Rand.

Beaguiles Were Blown And Drums Were Beaten,

Heralding The Imperial March;

Colonies In For A Big Surprise,

Found Reforms The Greatest Farce.

~.~

Great Depression Dented Nature,

Hand Of Cruel Fate Unfold;

Hitler, Mussolini And Stalin,

Harped On Simmering Got In Mold

Lamb Was Made Of Hailie Sallasie,

Harsh And Hot Grew Wild Winds;

De Gaulle, Churchill, Tojo, Hitler,

Made The World A Box Of Tinds.

Never Before The Shocks And Tremor,

Fumes And Fire Hit Space;

Bodies Count Lost Forever,

Boiling Seas With Mortal Mace.

Tojo's Raid On Pearl Of Harbor,

Shadow Roosevelt's Peace And Plan;

Silent Seas To See Turmoil,

Saddest Day Of Human Clan.

Deep's Of Ocean Craved For Breathing,

Hapless Humans Wept To Wane;

Heat Of Hell Was Everywhere,

None To Hear A Word Of Sane.

Hitler Overran All Europe,

Jews To Face The Holocaust;

Russian Boar The Brunt Of Fire,

None To Forget Ruthless Past.

Tragedy Had A Greater Tragedy,

Hiroshima With Atom Bomb;

Horror, Terror, Quake And Quivering,

Death Of Dance In Many A Womb.

Phoenix Of Peace Then Rows Up Slowly,

Out Of Furious Fuming Ash;

Ocean, Land And Woods Alike,

Felt The Shocks Of Fateful Bash.

~.~

Slavery A Curse Is Worst For Men,

A Slave Must Do What Masters Want;

The Slave Is Not Allowed To Think,

The Meanest Creature Like An Ant.

This Truth Went Home With Peoples Rise,

War Had Left Them High And Dry;

Kingdoms Crumbled Empire Broken,

Slave Bade Masters Well, Goodbye.

Star Of Freedom Rose In The East,

With Gandhi At The Helm Of Mast;

Mao The Maverik, Ho Chi The Hoary,,

Growing Nehru, Nesser's Caste..

Sleeping Lion Yawned A While,,

Winked To Find A Whole New Face;

Nkrumah, Nyerere To Kenyatta,

Kaunda, Mandela Won The Race .

Writers

Gift Of Language To Mankind,

Blooms In Full In Nature Notes;

Poets, Authors Or Playwrights,

Pave The Way For Time' Votes

Homer Sang The Sailors Glory,

Chancellor Excelled In His Tales;

Spencer's Queen Had Beautified,

Dismal World Of Dried Vales..

All In One And One Shakespeare,

Fanciful To 'hamlet' Cost,

Milton Moans Before The Maker,

Peeved At The 'paradise Lost'.

Wordsworth Hails The Beauteous Nature,

Coleridge Sings The 'mariners Rhyme',

'Prometheus' Plotting Still Shalley,

'Odes Of Keats' To Make One Of Mine.

Mad, Bad And Dangerous Darling,

Byron Billed As 'don Juan',

With All 'heaps Of Broken Images',

Eliott's Waste Land ' High For Quan.

Frost 'Boy' In Kipling's 'Jungle',

Sings 'Rubai' Of Khayyam,

Pope And Dryden Work Together,

Swift In 'Gulliver' Pushkin's Palm.

Tennyson Bets With Shots Of Canon,

Turns And Twists The Glorious War;

Ardent Optimism Of Browning,

Brings God In Cozy Car.

Arnold's Gypsy' Merman' 'Thyris',

Make A Point In Pessimism,

Hardy's 'Tess' A Pastoral Tragedy,

Loathes The Gods And Optimism

Thackery's Loss In 'Vanity Fair',

Esmond's Search Of 'Betrix Dove',

Whither To Find Wench Of Beauty,

Eyes Of Fire Looks Of Love.

Blake In Tandem Makes A Cry,

For The 'Songs Of Innocence',

'Tiger Tiger Burning Bright,'

Telling Us To Talk Up Sense.

~.~

While Shaw In 'Widower's House',

Brooding Over The Wasteful War,

Race Of Arms And Fields Of Murder,

Man Will Find A Deep Scar.

Crimes Motive Search To Find,

Where The Criminal Runs And Roams,

Lot Of Labor Lost In Reason,

Off With Doyle's Sherlock Holmes.

'Dorien Grey', A Paint Of Wilde,

H.G. Wells In 'Time Machine',

Ibsen's 'Ghost' For Balzac Right,

'Island Treasure' Rl Stine.

Duma's 'Muskets' Set Aside,

Dante Did Give Heart And Soul,

''Quixote' Quickly Hitting Windmill,

Cervantes A Role Model.

~.~

Oliver Wages Lonely Battle,

Dickens Find A 'Bleak' In World,

'Crusoe' Defoe's Only Hero,

Chats Too Wild With Hair Curled

Hugo's 'Hunchback' Gets A Scare,

Hearing Fairy Andersen Tales,

Crime And Punishment Meets Of 'vsky,

In 'Cabin Tom' With Stowe Sales.

Tolstoy Royal Saint A While,

Harnessed Working 'War And Peace',

Bursting Shells With March Of Matter,

Shows The Tragic End Of Greece.

Science and Progress

Pastoral Man In Hunting Stages,
Flies Fast In Aeroplanes;
Woodland Huts To Skyscrapers,
Lost In Thoughts Of Memory Lanes.
Ptolemies Hit With The Solar System,
Copernicus's Revolving Plan,
Arybhatts Celestial Bodies,
Gali's Fixing The Sun's Span.
Keeper Watched The Planets Moving,
New Thesis For Modern Man,
Search And Find Space Is Wide,
Fly As Far As You Can.
Printing Owes To Guttenberg Right,
Bursting Learning Far And Wide
Knots Of Books With Common Mind,
Thoughts And Actions Turn The Tide.

~.~

First-time Germs Were Seen With Eyes,

Jansen Made The Microscope,

Gave All Doctor's Help Like

Final Word A Decree Of The Pope.

Newton Saw An Apple Falling,

What Made It Come To Earth?

Brooding Brought Gravity Light,

Planets Pull Is All It's Worth.

Body Aches With Fierce Fever,

No Measure For Rise And Fall;

Fahrenheit Made The Meter,

Doc's Stature True And Tall.

Only Rich Could Clad In Proper,

'fore The Crompton's Spinning Mule;

Clothe The World A Rising Slogan,

Dream Came True As Nature's Rule.

Stitching Cloth With Thread And Needle,

Sapped Energy Of The Artisan Clan,

Sewing Machine By How's Labor,

Boomed The Boon For Common Man.

~.~

A New Dawn Came To The Western Side,

Faraday With His Noble Flan;

Lead The Dark Of World To Light,

Electricity In The Right Span.

Then Appeared The Real Master,

Deaf Edison A Hundred Score;

Changed Life Of Our World Altogether,

The Electric Bulb To Diners Pores.

James Watt Saw Castle Boiling,

Found The Fierce Force Of Stream;

Chook Chook Engine Ran While

Railway Fast To Show It To Gleam.

Sending Messages Eased The Burden,

Morres Touch With Telegraph;

Graham's Phone A Ring In Tandem,

Turning Sputter In Electrograph

Waves Of Radio Marconi Mumble,

Thompson's Electron Drew The Plan;

Jean's Cinema To Baird's Tv,

Filled Our Race With Bubbles Of Elan

Age of Exploration

Icarus The Pioneer Age Of Venture,

Burnt His Wings In Lap Of Death;

Risk Becomes The Zest Of Life,

Bears The Brunt Of Godly Rap.

Fi-huan, Huent-sang, Crossed The Himalayas

Marco Polo To Modern Land

Ibn-batuta A Desert Dweller,

Reached A Court At Golden End.

Henry Hero The Navigator,

Lent Men A Helping Hand,

Oceans Boomed With Gutsy Sailors,

Searching Land In Gritty Bands.

Columbus, A Euro Hero,,

Sailed To Find The Indian Shore;.

Ended Up In Western World

Searching For New Worlds More And More.

Vasco De Gama Took A Round,

Cape Of Good Hope Lured The Rope;

A Hard Day's Labor Worth Its Find,

Indian Platter As A Sop

Drake And Magellan Sailed Together,

Proved The Point That Earth Is Round;

Amerigo's March From North To South,

Sizzling New World He Had Found.

Quest Of Cook On Lonely Ocean,

Found Him On Last Of Land;

'neath The Weight Of Solid Ice,

Not A Trace Of Simmering Sand..

Heycrdahl's Kontiki Adventure,

Took Peru To Poly'sia Shore;

Pierry, Scott On Pole Tighter,

Wondered What A Land To Bore. .

Taboo Land African Wild,

Feared Most To Fill Folklore;

Livin'tone Left Comforts Rare,

Kith And Kin To Dark Explore.

~.~

Orville Wright, Wilbur Wright,

Gave The World The Greatest Gift;

Planes In Air Fast And Fair,

Made The Journey Quick And Swift

Age Of Venture To New Heights,

Zeppelin Flew Around The World;

Lindbergh To Not Lag Behind,

Flew Atlantic Solo Curled.

Hillary, Tenzing Climbed Miles,

Putting Feet On The Roof Of Earth;

Moon To Mars And Mars To Jupiter,

Range Of Man Is None To Dearth.

Violent Peace

Serve The Men To Serve God,

A Golden Rule For The ‘sapien Race;

Swelling Rank Of Monks And Minion,

Led The Luring Cast Of Mice.

Calvin, Luther Showed The Light,

Handed It To Joan Of Arc;

Kant And Gandhi,Roma, Roland,

Bore The Torch In Pitch Of Dark.

Martin Luther, Albert Schweitzer,

Gave Lead In Darkest Land;

Serving Here Serving There,

Soothed Sick And Weary Band.

Scene Of Battle Full Of Bodies,

Crying People Filled The Dale,

Treat The Wounded, Soreness Suffering,

Mercy Name Is Nightingale.

Baton In The Grip Of Theresa,
Charity Sister Stole The March;
Leper, Dying, Sick And Soaring,
'ma Was There On The Barge.
Peace For Men And Man For Mercy,
Always Prime To Russell's Plan;
War A Monster All The Time,
Ready To Swallow The 'sapien Clan.
Merrymakers Keep In Mind,
World Had Had Some Deep Scars;
Tremor, Terror, Fire, Famine,
Played Much Havoc With Wars.
Race To Power, Plan To Conquer,
Exploiting The Common Man;
Rulers With Haughty Air,
Rob The People As Much They Can.
Rage Against The Colonies System,

Brought Revolt In New New Land;

George, Messiah, Father, Freedom,

Painted At Rolling Heads On Sand.

~.~

Bourbon Branded Reign Reaction,

Spilled Blood In People's Name;

Dante, Robei, Mara, Madam,

Hands With Gore To Get Defamed.

'lution Hungry For Her Children,

Ate Them Up And Turn Of Own;

Sick And Weird Thing The Guillotine,

Call Them In With Loud Moans.

Czars' Russia In Same Twilight,

Saw The Rising Common Folk,

Hungry Masses Turned The Tide,

Blood And Blood With Ground Soaked.

Reign Of Terror Everywhere,

Checka Settled Old Score;

Lenin, Trot, And ‘talin Roaring,

Bath In Blood On Every Door.

Changes Rule The Rolling Planet,

Olden Gives The New A Chance;

Sordid Tales Of Harrowing Data,

Leaves The Grip For Lighter Lance.

Beauty in Art

Art And Music, Love And Nature,

Acts On Wounds As Soothing Balm.

Crux Of Matter Always Loading,

Human Soul With Quiet And Calm.

Beethoven Bore The Brunt Of Music,

Tinged The Spirit, Mind And Soul;

Gave Relief To Tragic Life;

Never Waver From The Goal.

Mozart, Master Of Mystical Melody,

Concert Giant Opera Sung;

Requiem Mass For End Of Life,

Penniless Rich But Died Young.

Hucbald, Arezzo Machant Singer

Soprano, Alto, Tenor, Bass

Stephen Foster, Wagner, Bardi

Purcell, Handel, Gluck And Bach.

~.~

Painters' Father Botticelli,

Pagan Love To Myth And Rhythm

Birth Of Venus Coronations,

Primavera With Art Of Cythm.

Michael's Angels Family Holy,

Sistine Chapel, Vatican Rome;

Moses And The Bound Captives,

Judgement Last In Every Home.

Marriage Of Virgin, Piece Of Raphael,

Soothing Every Nerve Of My Heart;

Love And Eternal Source Of Life,

Alba Madonna The Highest Art.

Girogine Plays The Pastoral Symphony,

Sleeps With Venus And Idyllic Scene;

Lover Of Nature Lover Of Beauty,

George The Great Is Full Of Sheep.

Vinci All In One In Sight,

Last Supper With Florence Guild;

Mystery Smiles Mona Lisa,

Machine The Flight Did He Built.

A War So Cold

End Of War In Cold Images,

Threat Of Blocks To Fragile Peace;

Commis And Capitals, Locked In Fight,

Tremor, Tension, Terro's Niece.

John Kennedy Showed His Might,

Khrushchev Withdrew Warlike Plans;

Indira Gandhi, Goldamier,

Female Power Joining Clan.

Peace Elusive All The Time,

Gangs Of Goons In Post War Dawn.;

Mafia Raised A Hell Of Fire,

Al Capone And Ku Klux Klan

Harried Jews From World Around,

Finally Got A Space To Breathe;

Promised Land To Moses Maker,

Band Of Judea Growing Teeth.

~.~

Always From War And Genocide,

World Has Always Gleams Of Hope;

Best Of Science And Peer,

Handling The Man With Rarest Sop.

Gates Of New Fronts Found Open,

Gagarin's Entry Into Space;

Walk On The Moon A New Stride,

Neil, A Hero To Titan Race.

Religion and Despair

Butchering Souls In Name Of The Maker,

Fraud On Him Which Need To Blast;

Millions Sent To Gas Chambers,

Unparalleled A Holocaust.

Factory Gas, A Greater Killer,

Fills The Lungs With Poisonous Pall;

Hapless Human Bhopal Version,

Had The Real Yama's Call.

Greedy Gases Know No Bound,

Turn The Earth And Fatal Field

Chernobyl Plant Of Russia

Killed Thousands For A Yield

Name Of Allah Dragged It To Slaughter,

Thousands Of Peaceful Souls;

Bombing On The Ninth Of Eleven

Murky Deed With A Gory Goal.

Mother Nature Responds

Gilgamesh In El Dorado,

David Luring Khufu, Seti,

Yu Shun Gasps To Reach Cyrus,

Noah, Caesar Not In Jetty.

Missi, Nile, Thames And Rhine,

Congo, Tigris, Huangoho Seeping;

Dead Saraswati, Euphrates Sinking,

Only Lana, Zamzam Leaping.

Zambe Shows Some Sign Of Life,

Yangtze, Ganga, Volga Racing;

Darling Indus, Only Heavenly,

Fatal Destiny All Them Facing.

Too Much Blood Has Flown With Water

Danube Has To Make Reply,

Fuming, Foaming Amazon Roaring,

Mekon Asking Reason Why.

Rama, Krishna, Durga Sita

, Moses, Confucius,Mohamed, Issa

Buddha, Tao, Zorastria,

Toa, Veda, Bible, Gita

Ovid, Virgil, Horus, Homer,

Vyas With Kali, Tulsi Fear

Blind Milton, Deaf Beethoven

Crying Wild None To Here

Greek To Roma, To Vendal Bulgar,

Lydian, Goath , To Moor And Medes;

Hun, Mongol, Bedouin,Berber;

Spilling Blood And None To Heed.

Rulers of Earth

We Will Rule The World With Might,

Arms And Arms And Arms To Fight;

Keeping War To Shore Apart,

Making Every Wrong Right.

We Will Rule The World With Guile,

Cunning And Deceit For Mile And Mile;

Ours Is The Century You Must Note,

Move, And Move No Rest Awhile.

We Will Rule The World With Oil,

Forcing Dessert Rule And Toil;

Make The Weaker And Women Slave,

Crushing Umma Under Soil.

We Will Rule The World With Mast,

A Dye Is There To Be Cast;

Why A Babel To Rule Again,

When We Have Ruled The World In Past?

We Will Rule The World With Passion,

Buddha's Words And Yoga's Lesson,

Utopian Piece Of Ocean's Bottom,

Talk And Talk And Every Session.

~.~

Chanakya King And Machiavelli's Prince,

Dining Together While In The Ring,

"I", "My", "Me", And Mine,

The Only Rant They Like To Sing

Atlas, Carmel, Crystal, Fuji,

Rocky, Ida And Ural

Find Himalaya Horrified;

Huddle Together For A Wall.

The Atoms Turn Has Come At Last,

Only Whimpers, Not A Blast;

Turning Everything To Ashes,

Leaving Civility A Thing Of The Past.

Man Is Making A Fool Of Himself,

Always Talking Atomic Themes,

'Darkling Plain' And 'broken Images',

Peace Remains A Distant Dream

A Light In The Dark

Masses Lie For Self In Shadow,
Wait For Their End To Come;
Leader Lends Support To Life,
Never Works For Gain To Some.
He Is A Burning Candle,
Shedding Light To One And All;
Sorrow, Suffering, Have A Sacrifice,
Roll His Way To Make Him Fall.
He Does Not Waver, Nor Does His Favor
Firmly Stands To Face The Front;
Uses Wisdom, Face Of Future,
Always Ready To Bear The Brunt.
Sturdy Going, Always Saying,
Never Waiting For A Park;
Better To Light A Lamp Together,
Then To Make A Fuss Of The Dark.

~.~

Mother Earth Is Never Barren,
Nor Has She Won And Mints;
People Come And Go In Time,
Leaving The Ground With Imprints.
In Reams Of The Dark, A Gleam Of Light,
Growing Slowly To Take Flight;
A Day Will Come And Shine Bright,
To Make The Wrong Of Humans Right.
Buddha Will Meet Christ In Rome,
The Prophet Be There From The Dome
To Shake Hands With Moses And Tao
All In Eden To Share Some Som
Lincoln Will Rise From The Grave,

And Gandhi Make Sermons Again;
'Fucius Teaches Human Values,
Thomas More To Shun The Pain.
Among The Tales Of Death And Doom,
Life Never Fails To Bloom;
To Quote Keefe's Immortal Mind,
If Winter Come,
Can Spring Be Far Behind?

9 798885 910194

Printed by Libri Plureos GmbH in Hamburg,
Germany